that's curious

Kathy

Enjoy

Boyd McLeek

Scurfpea
Publishing

First edition 2019.

Cover art by Boyd McPeek, drawing, "Muse".

Scurfpea Publishing
P.O. Box 46
Sioux Falls, SD 57101
scurfpeapublishing.com
editor@scurfpeapublishing.com

that's curious

Artwork and Commentary
by
Boyd McPeek

— Page 54 from Sketchbook started Nov 13, 2017

Contents

The Traveler Surveys The Odd Structure

The traveler stopped on the path and surveyed the structure. "That's curious," he thought. The structure looked like it was alive. Leaves grew out of the roof and what looked like a bunch of fruit was hanging from the top. There were doors and windows and a winch sticking out of an upper turret. "I wonder who is responsible for this?" he thought as he walked to the door.

Chapter 1:
That's Curious

Curiouser and Curiouser! Cried Alice (she was so much surprised, that for the moment she quite forgot how to speak good English). – Lewis Carrol, Adventures in Wonderland

An artist friend suggested the title "Curiouser and Curiouser – The Curious Worlds of Boyd McPeek" for an art show I was planning. I liked the term "Curious." "Curious" describes my art as being a little quirky. It is not as strange as surrealism, but it is not realism either. It is a little different – like the characters Alice encountered in Wonderland.

I don't intentionally draw quirky stuff. Take the image on the previous page of the traveler surveying the odd structure. I didn't set out to draw that. I was having coffee and doodling in my sketchbook, like I do almost every day, when it just happened. I fell down a rabbit hole and things got curiouser and curiouser. The image started to look like a building with leaves, so I went with that and started adding stuff.

I'm not sure where the traveler came from. Suddenly he was just standing there looking at the odd structure. So, to answer the traveler's question: "I am responsible." I drew the odd structure with the fruit on top.

Most of my drawings start just like that — doodles that got out of hand. Occasionally, I set out to draw something specific, but usually not. If the doodle looks interesting, then I add bells and whistles — or doors and windows. Whatever works. Here is an example of a doodle that I haven't embellished much.

I first drew images like this in a one-room country school in Clark County. There was one teacher for eight students in six different grades. The school was twelve miles from the nearest town and a quarter mile from the nearest farm houses. Nature was literally right outside the door. Across the road was our favorite sledding hill in winter. In the spring, we went for nature hikes down the abandoned township road next to the school. This was where my interest in nature and the environment began.

My Dad was a conservationist because of his experiences growing up in the Dust Bowl. He planted tree strips on our farm to keep the dirt from blowing away. He tried alternative farming methods to reduce soil erosion and to build the soil. He showed me how we can take action where we live to protect the environment. You will notice environmental themes and comments throughout this book.

I think I was in fifth grade when the teacher taught us an art technique involving drawing a continuous line on a sheet of paper. Once you had a swirly, squiggly figure you filled in the spaces with hash marks, color and other embellishments. I loved this technique because I could draw freely and spontaneously, but still end up with an interesting piece of art. I soon saw animals and people in the shapes that I drew.

The front cover is an example of a doodle that turned into a figure with a face (the black oval). This image is as close as I come to symbolism. The figure is my muse or creative side. It is rising out of a book and looking at a curious structure with a fisherman on the porch.

The symbolism that the muse rises out of a book is important.

I come from a family of bookworms. Our farm house had a library of books — history books, adventure stories, kid detective books. There wasn't much to do on the farm, so we entertained ourselves by reading. I don't know where the books came from, but I read them all several times. The adventure books had a few pictures, but mostly I had to imagine what the author was describing — like the Swiss Family Robinson's tree house. Reading let me travel to desert islands and see strange beasts. That is probably what started me down this winding, faintly-marked path that led me here.

For this book, I went to my sketchbooks to find pencil drawings that were not too smudged or coffee-stained to use. Normally, I scan the images and use *Inkscape* (a vector graphics application) to make a vector graphic image. I then digitally color the image. This is how I did the illustrations for the books *World of If* and *Elsewhere* by Scurfpea Publishing.

But people enjoy the pencil sketches as well, so I decided to use only sketches for this book. I scanned the pencil sketches and cleaned up the smudges and other errata in the jpeg image using *Gimp* (Gnu Image Manipulation Program). It took a little practice to get the darkness and contrast values set right so that the digital images looked like the original pencil sketches.

I wrote the text and set up the manuscript in *LibreOffice* which is another open source (free) program. I inserted the jpegs into the document so I could see how the final document would look and how long it would be. I knew that my editor/publisher would set up the final document using professional layout software, so I didn't have to get it perfect.

As I assembled the pictures, I realized that I would need commentary about them. Some of the drawings were done years ago, so I didn't remember much about what I was thinking when I drew them. So, I made stuff up (which is called "fiction" when it is about odd pictures, otherwise it is called "lying").

So, on these pages you will find fictionalized accounts of what might be going on in a picture, as well as mostly-factual comments about why I drew it, etc. The contents are loosely organized into categories based on superficial similarities. Beyond that, everything is pretty random. There will be comments to explain particularly puzzling things – but some will defy explanation completely. Some commentary may strike you as "off the wall" because it is. You have been warned.

When you look at my images it is useful to think of them as existing in a galaxy far, far away, on some exoplanet with two moons in the sky. Even though physicists claim that the laws of physics are the same everywhere in the universe, I think I have found places where things are little different. You will understand why, when you see the pictures. I refer to this other-worldly concept as "Not From Around Here".

The image "The Alien" which I drew in 1976 after reading Frank Herbert's "Dune" is an example of this concept. This was my first close encounter with strange beings suddenly appearing in my drawings. It was such an interesting experience to see an unexpected image take shape that I knew I wanted to keep drawing like this just to see what else would materialize. Over the years, other shapes have materialized. The best ones are those that just happen without much conscious thought. Some of the best sketches were converted to digital images and appear in the books *World Of If* and *Elsewhere* and on aluminum prints. I no longer have the pencil sketches for those.

A grade school teacher told me I had a lot of imagination. I don't remember the context in which she said that, but I took it then, and remember it now, as a compliment. I had a ton of fun using my imagination to make this book. I hope you will enjoy it too.

You may get more out of this book if you exercise your imagination. For instance, when you look at an image of a building, like the odd structure at the front of the book, imagine yourself inside the structure. Pick one of the windows and imagine what the room behind it

The Alien

looks like. Does it have wood paneling on the ceiling and a dusty bookshelf with ancient volumes of forgotten lore? What is the view like looking out the window? If you were going to live in the house, which room would you pick as yours? Let your imagination roam the halls. Have fun.

You will find an additional feature scattered throughout these pages. I call it "Curious Comic".

People would say that not only is my art curious, so is my sense of humor. The Space Excursion picture on the next page was inspired by a *Monty Python* skit called *The Ministry of Silly Walks* in which John Clease stomped around with unusual gaits. In this image, a spaceman stomps around an exoplanet with unusual gaits. He is so very happy to be out of the habitat, away from certain crew members (it was a long voyage), that his exuberance shows. So, Curious Comics are random sketches with random thoughts as captions.

Please, get comfortable, sit back and look at the pictures. Laugh if you feel like it. Now that you know what to expect, lets head down a rabbit hole and see if we find anything curious.

Curious Comic

A Space Excursion

Chapter 2:
Tree-mendous

———————

The images in this section are based on a concept for creating houses from trees which I call *Grow Your Own Abode*. These tree houses and tree villages address the problems of deforestation and urban sprawl with one highly improbable solution – trees (really, really big trees).

I was walking in my neighborhood one day under beautiful boulevard trees, when I heard a voice say "Hi". I looked up and there in a big tree was a boy in a tree house. I guess he wanted to make sure that somebody saw him up there. The tree house was a large wooden platform with a roof, a handrail and a wooden pirate head on one end. It was a tree house and a pirate ship. A kid with an imagination could have a lot of fun up there.

That encounter started me doodling and researching tree houses. There are some fantastic tree houses out there – just search for "tree house" on the Internet. The best ones look like they grew out of the tree – like the owner planted a sapling and a few years later had a house. I explore that concept in the next few pages.

The Byrd House

When I doodle images, I don't worry about details. I just go for an interesting look. I drew this tree house with individual rooms on a big branch. When I finished it, I started thinking about the details — like how do you get from room to room? There seem to be several options: run along the branches like a squirrel, crawl through the branches if they are hollow or use winches and ropes to get pulled up through a trap door in the floor of the room. All of those options have drawbacks. The best option is to fly like a bird and land on the branch. . . so, obviously, I need to doodle alien bird-people with wings if I draw another house like this.

Twin Tree Village

With this image I made the branches bigger so there could be stairways inside. But if people don't want to go down one branch and up another to get to another unit, I added a special feature – zip lines! I'm sure kids would love that feature, but Grandma and Grandpa not so much.

This image is inspired by tree house resorts I saw on the Internet. In those, the guest rooms were actually in separate trees and most were held up by posts (I think that's cheating).

Tree Town in a Really, Really Big Tree

This is a tree town with a lot of buildings in a really big tree. There are stairs and elevators to get around in it. I added another special feature in this image. Well-designed communities have places for young people to get together and have fun, so I left a big space on the nearside of the tree for a really awesome skateboard park.

Bamboo Towers Tree Village

Bamboo is actually grass, but the title *Bamboo Towers Grass Village* could be misconstrued, so I changed it to *Bamboo Towers Tree Village.*

Curious Comic

Dad Takes a Shortcut

Chapter 3:
Porchiness

―――――――――――

These drawings display the property of "porchiness" – having extensive, unusual porches. Sitting on a porch on a summer day is a rewarding experience. Houses with porchiness maximize that summer breeze feeling.

Porches are a product of "vernacular architecture" in which buildings are designed to fit the local climate. Porches help shade the walls of a building to keep it cool in a hot climate. Lemonade and ice cream also keep us cool, but they came later.

Bungalows are a house design defined by the use of porches or covered entry ways. Bungalows come in many styles – Arts & Crafts, Chicago, Hacienda – but all have a porch . . . or an enclosed room where the porch used to be. I take long walks around my neighborhood just to see all the styles of bungalows. There is even a version with Sioux quartzite from local quarries for the porch supports and columns. So my exploration of "porchiness" begins with my take on the classic bungalow.

Twisty Post Style Bungalow

Why twisty posts for the porch supports? I was trying for a rustic, craftsman-style bungalow and nothing says "rustic" like twisty posts. So I went with twisty posts and a funky porch railing.

I drew a lot of images of bungalows with twisty posts, but this is the only one to make the cut.

Twin Porch Bungalow

This house has two porches with a bump-out in between that features a window seat. It's the perfect nook to read a book – one with curious porch pictures.

Twisty Post Gazebo

A porch without a house is a gazebo. Note the winch hanging from the ceiling. That is not normal for gazebos.

Really Tall Porch

In a finished version of this image, I added native plants like purple coneflower and bee balm to the front yard. The colorful blooms really added pop to the picture, just like native plants add pop to the ecosystem. Native plants were growing in every locale before humans arrived and had evolved along with native animals and insects. So, planting native plants helps native fauna, like butterflies, survive. Unfortunately, "wildflower" seed may not be native plant seed. Many plants called wildflowers are invasive species that have escaped and now grow wild. So be careful with seed or you will end up with weeds. To add habitat in the city, I planted my yard and the space between the sidewalk and street to native plants. It looks like a prairie meadow with bees, birds and butterflies.

The Long And Winding Porch

I set out to draw a long porch and this is what materialized. An earth-sheltered retirement home with a section of porch for each resident? If this is the south side of a passive solar structure, the porch could block the high summer sun from entering the building but let in the low-angled winter sun (assuming this structure is in the northern hemisphere of whatever exoplanet it is on). Passive solar is a little known way to get free energy. The basic concept of passive solar is to put windows where the sun can shine in when you want heat, but where sunlight is blocked when you don't want heat. Simple, huh.

Chapter 4:
Perchiness

A structure that clings courageously to cliffs has a quality called "perchiness" i.e. to perch precariously on a precipice. The inspiration for these images is probably the Buddhist monasteries in Tibet that are really perchy. They sit very high up on cliffs and look exotic and mysterious. On a perchiness scale of 1 to 10 they are 11. My version of a perchy monastery on a mountain top is on the next page along with commentary about who might live there. The other images are much tamer – a 5 or 6 on the perchiness scale. Let's take a look.

Perchiness ⟶

Order of Cardiovascular Adherents

The highest ranking adherents live on the top floor of the monastery. They are black-belt cardios who have completed a 1200 step program. Novices live on the first floor and meditate on if they really want to be black belt cardios.

Perchy House on the Beach at Low Tide

Living in this perchy house has its challenges. Notice that the floors seem to be slanted at about 30 degrees and getting to the front door requires a Sherpa – and that's when the tide is out! The good news is that no lawn care is required – except to recycle the plastic that washes in with the tide.

This drawing is another example of not thinking about the details when I drew the image.

Another Perchy House

This perchy house has a ground-floor entrance for people with acrophobia. There is also a roof deck without a handrail for those with anti-acrophobia.

Whenever I think my pictures are "way out there", I watch a few videos like "Extreme Homes". I only draw pictures – some people actually build weird homes in weird places. Trust me.

Perchy Roadhouse on the Moor

The wind was a torrent of darkness among the gusty trees.
The moon was a ghostly galleon tossed upon cloudy seas.
The road was a ribbon of moonlight over the purple moor,
And the highwayman came riding –
    Riding – riding –
The highwayman came riding, up to the old inn-door.
    – The Highwayman *by Alfred Noyes*

This is the first stanza of a long poem by Alfred Noyes, published in 1906. In this poem, "highwayman" refers to a bandit or outlaw. I love the imagery of the ghostly galleon and the ribbon of moonlight. I can't say for sure that the poem was the inspiration for this picture, but . . . let's go with that.

Perchy Hamlet On The Fjord

I have drawn a number of these villages perched on a cliff, but I'm not really happy with any of them. The perspective is tricky with all those roofs running in different directions. I'm trying for a maze of houses on several levels that are carved from the cliff. Then I want the cliffs to enclose a bay with a Viking-like ship anchored near an island in the center. I don't know where this vision came from, but it could make a good setting for a science fiction/fantasy story. To draw that, I will need a cup of really good coffee and a couple uninterrupted hours at my favorite coffee house.

Chapter 5:
Of Beasts and Barnyards

I grew up on a farm, so drawing beasts and barns is right up my alley. I came across a class project I did at the one-room country school I attended. My mother had saved it. It was a picture of Evangeline's calf. *Evangeline, A Tale of Acadie* is a poem by Henry Wadsworth Longfellow. I'm sure I should have gotten more out of the poem than the fact that Evangeline had a pet calf, but I was just a kid. I drew a picture of a calf because I could and got an A on the paper.

I continue to doodle animals for fun and relaxation. I have also read a lot of science fiction books, so some of the beasts reflect that "Not From Around Here" quality I talked about earlier.

Barnyard with Random Additions

This barn has several odd sections stuck together. The section on the right has a big door for loading hay into a hay mow, as it was called in the old days. Most of the old barns had a hay trolley that was used to hoist loose hay in a sling up into the hay mow. The trolley ran on a steel track mounted to the rafters and had pulleys and ropes to lift the hay. We never used the trolley on our farm. We just threw hay bales into the loft by hand, then dragged them back into the hay mow and stacked them. The bales were heavy. It was an involuntary fitness program that was pretty effective. I was in good shape when I was a kid. Those days are gone.

Granaries with Antique Wheelbarrow

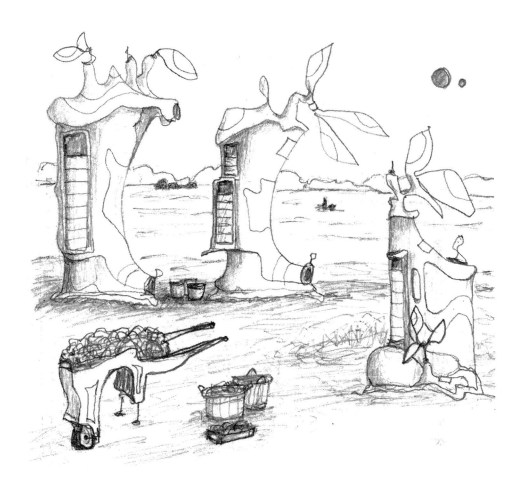

The granaries on our farm didn't look like this, but then, this is not our farm. Notice the two moons in the sky. These granaries are not from around here. They have what looks like a spout with a control handle to get the grain out. I had to shovel the grain out of our granary. Whoever built these understood work — like how to avoid it.

Three-Hump Herd Beast

This creature's home exoplanet doesn't have a good ozone layer, so evolutionary mutations occur frequently.

Outback Station

I only know about the Outback from Crocodile Dundee movies, but that didn't stop me. I drew this barn next to oddly-formed rocky outcrops and thought it looked like the Australian Outback. The two moons in the sky should have tipped me off that it wasn't in the Outback.

Barnyard with Beast of Burden

This barn has a hay loft and a silo and a beast of burden in the pen. There is also a cupola In the center. Cupolas provide ventilation for the barn and a home for annoying pigeons.

I drew a number of barns like this with sections pointing in different directions. They were tests to see if I could draw 2-point perspective without horizon lines and vanishing points like I learned in engineering school. I wanted to see if I could just wing it and get decent results. Tip: use curvy shapes to hide your mistakes.

Tall Horse

Salvador Dali's long-legged elephants influenced this image of a horse, although I did not take it to the "height" that he did. I "read" art books like the one about Dali's art for inspiration. That means I look at the pictures. The images are thrown into a junk room in my brain where they are jumbled together with other stuff I have collected. My muse rummages through the pile and sometimes pulls out something cool.

Bounty in Boxes and Bushel Baskets

Here are some more granaries with bushel baskets out front. These granary pictures were my attempt to represent October for a calendar I was working on (the only copy is hanging in my kitchen). The pictures are influenced more by the art of French Impressionists than by my experiences with harvest on the farm. On the farm, harvest was about tractors, combines and chaff blowing in my face.

On Mouse Patrol at the Granary

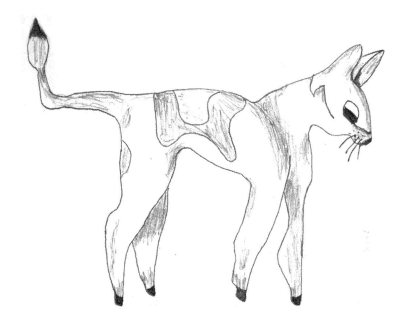

I can draw more realistic cats if I want to, but this just popped out of a doodle so I put it in here. He looks like he works out a lot.

Wheat Field with Crows – and Granaries

McPeek

Van Gogh's *Wheat Field with Crows* inspired this picture – the name, not the content. I just happened to put some crows in the picture, although you have to look closely to see them. You may also see gleaners out in the field, but that is a reference to another painting.

Shade Tree Barn

One last barn picture. This one has a curvy, organic look with a tree growing from the roof. I don't know why the tree is there, but I'm guessing it grows pretty well with all that organic fertilizer.

Curious Comic

Animal Adaptations

Chapter 6:
Life On Waterstreet

This next series of pictures is based on the theme of life in a swamp. The everglades are called the "River of Grass" because they are a river that has spread out over a large area of grass. It is not very deep in many places – just a series of swamps. So, that is the idea behind Waterstreet – a big swamp where roads are water and cars are boats. Think about that. No potholes to fill or snow to plow. No road construction detours all summer – sweet!

Muskrat Condos on Waterstreet

These muskrats got tired of plastering reeds with mud to make houses so they tried something new – 3-D printing. They either had a little trouble coding the printer app or they like *avant garde* architecture.

This image is another of those pictures I drew first and asked questions later – like "What the heck is this?" I followed this line of reasoning to come up with the muskrat connection – swamps are called sloughs up here in the Northland; sloughs have cattails or reeds; muskrats build lodges out of reeds so these must be muskrat condos.

Number Three Waterstreet

Also known as a high water house. It is a prototype for houses that adapt to rising water levels caused by climate change.

Mayor's House – Number One Waterstreet

The mayor's house shows that Waterstreet does not have any restrictive zoning laws. This block is zoned as "funky". You also don't have to worry about what you plant in your yard because there are no yards.

Notice the electric doorstep. When you arrive by boat, you step on the doorstep which is lowered to the dock. Then you recite a verse from your favorite poem. If the doorstep AI likes the poem, it raises you to the front door. Otherwise, it gives you a suggested reading list. ("AI" stands for artificial intelligence, which is different from the real kind).

Curious Comic

Mr and Mrs Wading-Bird Go to a Party

Chapter 7:
Beans and Baristas

Most of the images in this book were drawn in coffee shops. I will sit in a coffee shop for a couple of hours and draw. I meet people that way. They wonder what I'm doing and strike up a conversation. And, having the Barista call me by name when I walk in makes me feel like Norm on *Cheers*. So here is my tribute to the coffee shops, coffee roasters and baristas, both living and departed, who made this book possible.

Last Picture at Black Sheep Coffee
3/28/2017

McPeek

Summoning the Muse

This is my muse, Caffeinia. She is awakened by the aroma of freshly-roasted coffee. A muse is a "personified force who is the source of inspiration for a creative artist". She likes a light roast in a French press.

Still Life with Coffee Stain

This image is a still life. I try my hand at different styles of art, and what better subject than an aromatic cup of brew and a unique coffee pot. The unique coffee pot accounts for the stain on the table cloth. The pot looks a little bit like the teapot in *Alice In Wonderland*. Hmmmmm.

Connections

Coffee houses are frequented by artists, poets and other creative types. I met the publisher of this book in an artist-friendly coffee house. Through that association, I met many poets and artists and had my art and poetry included in several books.

The baristas who serve up coffee and lattes are often creative people themselves. Many have art backgrounds and do creative things in their off time. Mostly, they are just fun to talk to and will do a smiley face in your latte if you ask nicely.

In a coffee shop, I met a poet who has a following on Instagram. He pairs his poems with the artwork of people from around the world. I sent him an image that I thought fit his style. My pencil sketch and the poem he wrote for it are on the next page. His name is Lyle Hutchinson.

And join me now
As I lead you
Into quieter moments
Where time stills
And all that aches & pains you
Now and forever flees
Under the shroud lid-lined
night
Becoming the rest of ever

Your once longed-for
Peaceful rest
Delivered now
Born Reality
Of your own love's
Protective light

LWH
04-12-18

At Black Seahorse

We found this funky coffee house on the beach. See the three guys on the left? I'm the one in the middle. We talked about poetry, art, music, politics and other failings of human beings. The coffee was smooth with notes of toffee and chocolate. Coffy, the barista, is an artist too. We looked at photos of her work on her smart phone. Her abstract paintings are pretty dramatic and she knows who Jackson Pollock is!

This image, unlike most of my images, was constructed rather than just happening. I wanted to have three guys, a couple of baristas and a coffee machine in it. I tried ram's heads and dragon heads on the end of the counter, but decided to use the seahorse when I put the coffee house on a beach.

Coffee Roaster in the Wild

This image is my interpretation of a coffee roasting oven with its own coffee tree dropping coffee beans into the hopper. Of course, that is not how coffee gets roasted. Coffee roasters (people) use roasting ovens to roast the beans at just the right temperature and for just the right length of time to produce the great coffee that ends up in my cup. Coffee roasting is as much art as science. The smell of the beans and how they look while roasting tells the coffee roasters when the beans are ready. So, my salute to the coffee roasters who make the magic happen is "Cool beans".

Mug Shots

Chapter 8:
On the Desert Road

Deserts, camel caravans, remote oasis and mysterious travelers have given me lots of ideas for pictures. The images are loosely (very, very loosely) based on the history of the Silk Road. This was the route that brought silk from the Orient to Europe. I transposed the desert road idea to a distant galaxy where things are a little different. All the figures have dark ovals for faces. You can decide what they look like. The animals have faces, but they are not the usual donkeys and camels. Keep reading to see what I mean.

The Trader Reaches the Oasis

This is the first image I drew when I started doodling desert pictures. It is a rough sketch that I later turned into a digital image. Once I captured the idea of a trader reaching an oasis, I didn't spend any more time finishing the sketch. The pack beasts became pack birds in the digital image and the smudge by the tree became a pond. A picture of the pack bird is on the next page.

Desert Pack Bird

The Pack Bird is based on an image from a Buck Rodgers story. The original image showed a French Foreign Legionnaire riding a big bird. I turned the steed into a pack bird so I didn't have to explain what a Legionnaire was doing in my picture.

Wireless Beast of Burden

Caravanserai

Caravanserai were walled enclosures on the Silk Road where caravans could circle the wagons at night. Of course, they had camels, not wagons. *Caravanserai* is also the name of one of my favorite *Santana* albums.

Caravan Master

Desert Scout

Trader with Mulephant Pack Beast

A mulephant looks like a mule but has a trunk like an elephant. I don't know why.

Water in the Desert

Palm Tree Oasis

This is a desert tree village with rooms for rent. Caravans park in back.

Chapter 9:
Pointy Houses

I have drawn so many of these pointy houses with appendages growing out of the roof, that you would think I know exactly what I'm trying to draw. The thing is, I don't have any idea what those things could be. They don't look like TV antenna or lighthouse beacons. Maybe they are some alien high tech gadgets whose use will become clear when we reach enlightenment . . . many, many years from now.

Pointy House on the Dock of the Bay

On this pointy house, the things on the roof could be wind generators. Unfortunately, the wind doesn't seem to be blowing in this image, so we still don't know what they are.

Pointy House on the Point

Here, the things on the roof are facing each other.
Curious.

Pointy House on the Point with Boat

Here, the gizmos are still facing each other, but are close together. Does that mean something?

Maybe the things on the roof are cosmic ray receptors that give the inn's signature Cosmic Coffee Cake its out-of-this-world flavor. Maybe. It's a theory.

Pointy Pair

The other pointy houses were on water, but this one is plunked down in the middle of nowhere. It has a companion that could be a pointy house wannabe. They both have appendages of uncertain purpose growing from the roof, but they are a little different. Why? The pointy house mystery deepens.

Are These Pointy Houses ?

Spooky Pointy Houses on the Dunes

Curious Comic

Looking For The Source of Mysterious Signals

Two Explorers Make A Startling Discovery

Chapter 10:
Inexplicable

My sketchbooks are loaded with pictures that are just inexplicable. I don't know where they came from, what they are or where they are going. They are just shapes which may resemble something real or they may be an illusion. You decide.

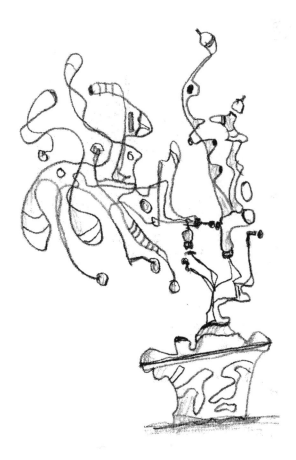

Yard Art Gone Curious

A steam-punk space capsule, 1940-ish gas pump, horse weather vane and ???. Totally inexplicable.

Shapes on a Sandbar

I expanded my horizons with this drawing. It is still inexplicable, but now it could be a landmark for that ship on the horizon.

More Connections

There are more inexplicable images on the next page. It is not easy creating captions for inexplicable images. Here are captions I wrote for the images: *Channeling Tim Burton, Alone on An Island* and *Dial Me Up, Scotty*. You can match the captions to the pictures anyway you want – or you can make your own caption.

One aspect of writing this book that has fascinated me, is the different interpretations people have for my drawings. Since I often don't know what these drawings are about myself, I welcome explanations from others. I was at a coffee shop showing the images on the next page to Lyle, the poet we met earlier. He writes about relationships a lot and had this take on the sequence of images:

In the top drawing, the two figures are looking off in different directions as if they were alone on an island (oops, now you know the caption I had for that picture).

In the middle image, the figures are together in that spooky place where relationships form and may also dissolve.

Finally, the relationship survives and solidifies, They have it "dialed in".

When I looked at the images and saw that sequence, I thought "How the heck did that happen?"

Inexplicable And Beyond

Door To Inexplicability

On the surface, this image seems inexplicable, but if you look at the clues you come to a surprising conclusion. The clues are: a massive door on a small structure that might be an entrance to an underground chamber; a periscope; what could be a vertical axis wind turbine; something that looks a little like a jukebox; and alien graffiti. When you put the clues together, you realize that this is an alien, subterranean, wind-powered, rocking disco!

Here I am
Prayin' for this moment to last
Livin' on the music so fine
Borne on the wind
Makin' it mine
>   — Night Fever, *the BeeGees*

Chapter 11:
Mother of Inventions

They say that necessity is the mother of invention. Well, these images weren't necessary, but they do show unintended inventiveness. Harnessing the wind to reduce reliance on fossil fuels is a big deal, so I have my version of a wind generator. There are also derricks, boats and something else. The other inventions may be solutions looking for problems.

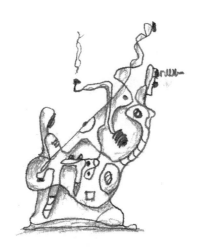

Wind Generator

The thing on the left is the wind generator. It is based on a real generator concept. In this design, the wind blows in the openings at the top and is channeled down the tube. The Venturi Effect increases the wind speed. The gizmos at the bottom are my version of Tesla turbines to generate electricity from the air flow.

Dueling Derricks

This is not an open pit mine. It is something else. That's all I know. Someone suggested that the pit is a crater filled with water or some other liquid. These derricks are a little over-built if all they do is lift a 5 gallon bucket of water out of a crater.

African Queen Redux

I didn't realize that I was channeling the *African Queen* movie until I tried to write a caption for this image. The bulging shape on the cabin roof must be the steam boiler. Any second now, Humphrey Bogart will pop out of the cabin and start tinkering with it.

Thermodynamics at Work

This image really needs an explanation. Unfortunately, I don't have one. Maybe the three birds on the power line know something. (Note: Thermodynamics is the science of heat flow in engines, refrigerators and even distillation devices. The Second Law of Thermodynamics says my coffee will cool off if I don't drink it right away. We all know that, but they made it a law . . . so now it is official.)

Floater

This floater uses helium gas bags to keep it aloft above the runaway greenhouse atmosphere of Venus — or Earth in a few centuries.

"Sweet Dreams and Flying Machines"
– James Taylor

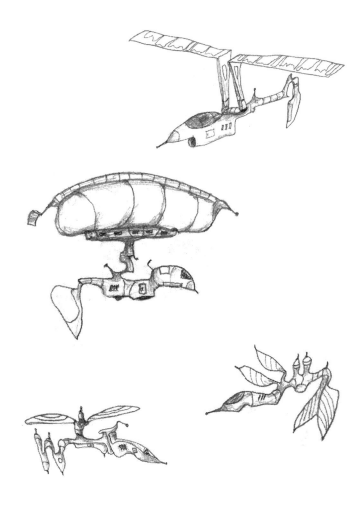

OK, I know the line is "Sweet dreams and flying machines in pieces on the ground" but I thought, what if they put the pieces together and flew them! What would they look like? This is probably not what James Taylor had in mind when he wrote the lyric. To fly, these machines must use advanced technology or the laws of physics must be replaced by magic.

I know this isn't an invention in the usual sense, but I think it shows inventiveness. Have you ever seen an image of an African antelope created with the letters of its name? I like to think I invented this art form, but actually it has been around for a while. It is called "letter art" or "text art". I drew a bunch of these with the thought of doing an alphabet book — but then I got to X. Quick, name an animal that starts with X.

Chapter 12:
Musicality

I have always loved music. Unfortunately, I don't have one musical bone in my body. I thought I did, but x-rays showed that it was just a calcium deposit. So, I do what I am capable of – listen to music and draw pictures based on incompletely-understood musical idioms. Musical instruments are fun to draw because they are swoopy (a colloquialism for organic-curvy-shaped). So here are some curious musical images.

Perchy Pizzicato

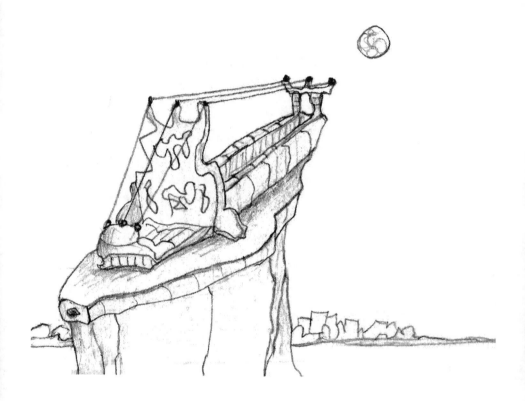

For the concert, frets on stanchions are installed under the strings. Musicians with hooked poles stand near the bridge to pluck the strings. Other musicians with padded tips on hooked poles run up and down the center aisle to press the strings to the frets to produce the notes. The conductor stands at the far end to direct the mayhem. When the moon lines up with the axis of the instrument, they play the *Moonlight Sonata.*

WARNING: Off the wall content alert. Take a deep breath and say "oooooooommmmmmmm".

Waiting for the Maestro

This image features a steam calliope, harp, drums, keyboard and a composer app on the cellphone. There is also a painter app that paints a picture of the music. If I knew anything about instruments, I probably wouldn't have put this combination together. The printer app may freeze up trying to paint the music.

Improbable Instruments

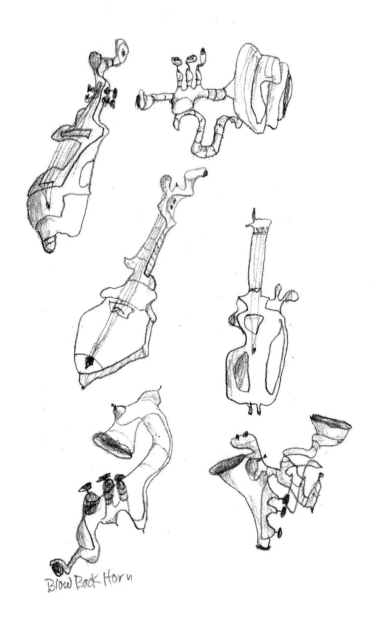

Blow Back Horn

Instruments played by the ExoPlanet Jazz Orchestra.

Chapter 13:
Village Life

I live in what I like to think of as a village near the center of a city. I can walk to two coffee shops (very important), a drug store, restaurant, my barber shop and the bank. If I put on my good walking shoes, I can walk to a grocery store, the food coop and a hardware store. Walking not only is good exercise, but it reduces pollution from driving. It may be a tiny bit of pollution reduction for one person, but if you multiply that times millions of people, we are talking real change! So one theme of the village images is walkability. Other themes are sustainability, community and, of course, oddity.

Village Kids

I drew this village with a narrow lane winding through it. It is a walkable village since cars have to go slowly down the lane. You can see kids playing in the lane. One of the kids is on the roof of a structure. "Why is he up there?" you ask. Because kids will be kids wherever they live. That is a good reason to have safe, walkable neighborhoods.

Life In The Slow Lane

This is a sketch that I turned into a finished image. I added shading to the digital image rather than shading the pencil sketch, so the sketch is a little light. The houses are inspired by shells. In this case, they must be the discarded shells of local escargot. You can see one in the foreground getting out of town at about 90 iph (inches per hour). He is taking advantage of the village's walkable design, though I'm not sure snail locomotion is called walking. In any case, using recycled materials must give the houses a good LEED* rating.

* Leadership in Energy and Environmental Design

Adobe Village

These adobe houses, camouflaged by gnarly trees and gnarly rocks, are examples of vernacular architecture and are made from a great local material: mud. The adobe (mud) absorbs heat during the day to keep the interior cool. It releases this heat at night when the desert cools off. This is heating and air conditioning without a plug-in and without contributing to global warming. Desert dwellers have been using this technology for millennia.

Row Houses

I was thinking about alternative housing styles when I drew this. We need more high density housing in the city, but who wants drab, industrial-looking apartments. If the residents could design their own units, they might look something like this. The eclectic design could build a strong sense of community because there is no place like their place anyplace.

Alien Architecture

Sprawly

I originally wanted to do a book on alien architecture, but changed my mind. I used some of the terms I coined for alien architecture in this book — like *perchy* and *porchy*. *Sprawly* is another such term. It means "to spread horizontally in a haphazardous fashion". Unfortunately, most cities today are really sprawly and that is not a good thing. Urban sprawl causes loss of habitat since open land is paved over. Air pollution also increases as people drive further to work or shop. This village, on the other hand, does not have cars, so it will stop growing when the walk to the cantina becomes too long.

Unincorporated

This village is unincorporated. That means it isn't really a village – just a cluster of houses. Their Director of Planning, Willy Nilly, prefers an unstructured approach to street layout. The inhabitants like its informal vibe and its walkability. It would be bike-friendly, too, if anyone owned a bike.

Long House Village

Maine long houses inspired this sketch. Long houses were a house that was connected to a barn by sheds to form one long structure. Farmers could get to the barn to feed their livestock without having go outside during snowy Maine winters. This structure looks more like sheds strung together than a house and barn. Here, again, I didn't work out any details before I drew this, although I did put a door in the center.

Village Square

The inspiration for this sketch was the concept of creating community gathering places by putting art in public areas. Where I live, there is an 18-foot-tall statue of a naked man with a slingshot in a park by the river (a bronze reproduction of Michelangelo's *David*). The statue caused controversy when it was installed in this very Midwestern town many years ago. Now, we have embraced public art and have a very nice Sculpture Walk downtown every year.

The statue in my sketch is more confusing than controversial because it is done in an Inexplicable style. I was trying to show a gathering place in the center of a village where people could meet and enjoy art.

Curious Comic

Exploring Exoplanets with Untested Technology

No signs of Life from the BioDetector

Chapter 14:
Drawings Bear Fruit

———————————

Page 14 in the sketchbook I started on November 13, 2017, is special. It is one of the two or three pages in the sketchbook that are not all scribbled up with half-finished, abandoned drawings or big smudges. It has six drawings that are all pretty clean and presentable. I used two of the drawings in the Desert Road chapter. I decided to put the other four drawings here, just to commemorate the occasion.

At the beginning of the book, we met the traveler who was staring at an odd structure with fruit on top. In this chapter, I revisit that theme to see what else I can come up with. These images reflect the "Grow Your Own Abode" theme I talked about earlier. In this case, the plant not only provides shelter, it also provides sustenance. A win-win.

Another Traveler, Another Odd Structure

I think this is a different traveler — he's dressed differently and stands a little shorter. The structure he is approaching is not very elaborate, but it has the tell-tale fruit on top that makes it an odd structure. Interestingly, the traveler seems to be looking at the house next door. I wonder what that looks like?

All Bunched Up

This house has two bunches of fruit on top. That organic fertilizer really works. Notice the three round things in the front yard — raised beds similar to the ones I built for my garden. There are some in the previous image as well. They work great for growing vegetables among the native plants in my yard.

Back At The Ranch

I don't know what to say about this image. The structure isn't as tall as the others, so I think of it as a ranch-style home. Ranch-style homes were popular after World War II. Houses were needed for all the babies in the Baby Boom years. While I am a card-carrying member (Social Security card) of the Baby Boom, I did not live in a ranch-style home until my late wife, Janet, and I bought our first house in the Twin Cities.

It was long and low, barn red and had shake siding. It did not have a bunch of fruit on top, but it did have a mulberry hedge around three sides of the property. We had lots of mulberries (jelly, jam, purple fingers, bird fertilizer on the ground). Maybe having purple fruit everywhere is where I got the idea for houses that produce fruit.

Bountiful Harvest

This is the last image from page 14. It looks like the other odd structures, but doesn't have fruit on top. You are probably thinking "What's up with that?" Well, I don't know. But since I am making stuff up after I did the drawing, anything goes. So, here is my take on the missing fruit.

It is harvest time. The fruit is ripe and ready to be used. Imagine yourself as the home owner. The bunch of fruit is taller than you and each berry is the size of a musk melon. How do you process it? Do you put each berry in its own giant-sized Bell jar with a pint of sugar to make jam? How about stomping on it in a big vat to make a fermented beverage? Or, you could dehydrate it to make fruit leather (the leather would be about the size of a cow hide). I'm sure with your imagination you can come up with more and better ideas — right?

Chapter 15:
Last Coffee House

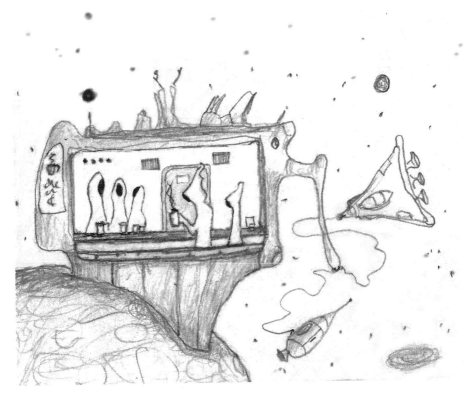

Well, we made it through the swamp, across the desert, past the pointy houses and down a village lane. Now, we find ourselves in a tiny coffee house on an asteroid. It is small, but the coffee is good and it has a great view of the Milky Way. To get here, we passed a lot of stuff that was pretty goofy or improbable and probably not from around here. I tried to keep things light-hearted, but there are references to problems we face on this planet — like climate change, poorly designed neighborhoods and loss of natural habitat. These seem like big problems that someone else will have to address, but there are things that we can do right here in River City to make a difference.

For instance, we can reduce loss of wildlife habitat by planting native plants in our yards. We call those strips of land between the sidewalk and street, boulevards. I had a vision one day while I was out walking — a Butterfly Boulevard. I have native plants in my boulevard and several of my neighbors have native plants in their boulevards. If people all over the city planted native plants, we could create a swath of natural habitat. Migrating birds and butterflies would have food sources and habitat all the way across town. A Butterfly Boulevard.

If we can make our neighborhoods more livable for butterflies, we can also make them more livable for people. I live in a quiet neighborhood where kids ride their bikes in the street and walk to school. It is not like that in many neighborhoods. Some streets are so wide and the traffic moves so fast that it is unsafe to walk or ride a bike. It doesn't have to be like that. City planners have discovered how to design streets to slow down traffic and make them safer for walkers and bikers. In the process, they found that slower traffic actually helped the businesses along the street because drivers had time to see what was there and were more likely to stop at those businesses.

Having walkable and bike-friendly neighborhoods can help us address the elephant in the room – climate change. A large contributor to climate change is automobile emissions. There are coffee shops and other stores within walking distance from my house. Whenever I walk to one of these places instead of driving my car, I help reduce auto emissions. If you drive less and walk or bike more, you can reduce emissions too. Millions of people driving to the store went a long way toward creating the greenhouse atmosphere, so millions of people walking to the store can help fix it. If your neighborhood isn't walkable, join or start a neighborhood association to see if you can change that.

It is completely obvious that climate change is affecting us here and now and we need to do something about it. Finding solutions will require that we actually commit to doing something and work together to do it. I hope that sensible people will step up and do what they can to solve the problem.

Astronomers estimate that there are more planets in the Milky Way than there are stars. So far, we haven't found any that seem to support life. Even if we found a habitable planet around the nearest star, it would take over a hundred years just to get there. So, as far as we can tell, we are sitting in the last coffee house in the Milky Way. In other words, we need to fix things where we live – here and now. We need to make it work and we can make it work.

Now I'm going to put my soapbox away and go out for coffee – to someplace unusual.

Acknowledgments

Thanks to Cathleen Benberg who provided the inspiration for the title of this book. I also want to thank her for her help and encouragement with my art projects over the years.

Lyle Hutchinson not only provided a poem for the book, he also reviewed the book and offered helpful suggestions. Lyle listened to me at the coffee shop as I struggled to express what I was trying to do with the book. Thanks Lyle.

My sister, Lois Peterson, reviewed the book and helped me clarify some issues. She also caught my references to things that happened during our childhood on the farm, proving that I didn't make everything up. Thanks Lois.

Steve Boint made this book possible by starting a writer-and-artist-friendly publishing company called *Scurfpea Publishing*. This has provided opportunities for myself and other local writers and artists. He also edited and did the layout for this book. Thanks, Steve.

Finally, I want to acknowledge all the people who stop to look at my pictures and talk to me at the coffee shops. You know who you are. Thanks.

About the Artist

Boyd McPeek grew up on a farm in Clark County, SD. A teacher at the one-room country school he attended taught him how to doodle a picture with one continuous line. That became his drawing style. He learned about perspective in drafting classes at the South Dakota School of Mines and Technology. That and a community-education watercolor class is the only art training he has had.

Even though Boyd has been drawing all his life, he didn't start displaying art work until about 2001 at the now-closed Horse Barn Art Center in Sioux Falls. The first art pieces he displayed were wood carvings called Worrywood. They were small animal figures with holes to allow twirling them on your finger. Later, he displayed wood sculptures made from boxelder and other wood found in and along the Big Sioux River.

In 2009 he discovered scalable vector graphics (svg) – a computer language that allows converting pencil sketches into computer images. He actually wrote code to make the first images. Now he has apps for that.

In 2010, Scurfpea publisher Steve Boint paired Boyd's drawings with Charles Luden's poems in a book called

World Of If. In 2014, his drawings were paired with the science fiction poetry of Steve Boint in a second book called *Elsewhere.* Boyd has had poems published in several anthologies and currently has wood sculpture and aluminum prints in Sioux Falls galleries.

Art has never paid the bills, so Boyd had day jobs. He worked in insurance loss control, as the safety director for a manufacturing company and, finally, as a business process analyst. That involved data mining on huge databases and creating computer applications to automate manual processes.

Now he is retired and living the dream — hanging out in coffee houses and drawing pictures. He also finds time to work with groups involved in public food forests, livable cities, local food and farming, food co-ops and benefit corporations.

Bonus Poem

Cold

Snow drifts down a brittle sky
and eddies restlessly over frozen ground.
The world is cold.
Stand at the bus stop
and feel the chill
in my bones – cold.
But those crows don't care.
Their raucous caws shatter
the icy air
at dawn
like a street gang
kicking over garbage cans.
I have no reply.
I pull my cap down against
the cold.

– Boyd McPeek

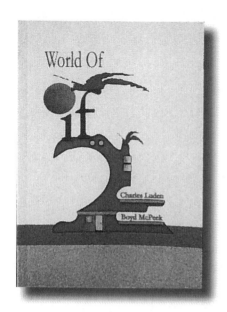

World of If

Neo-Zen poetry paired with McPeek's unique art produces a work of joyous meditation.

Elsewhere

Each piece of McPeek's artwork accompanied by a poem stands as a complete short story in verse. Elsewhere returns the wonder to science fiction.

Made in the USA
San Bernardino, CA
15 August 2019